WORKING

PLACES

**For a free color catalog describing Gareth Stevens'
list of high-quality books and multimedia programs,
call 1-800-542-2595 (USA) or 1-800-461-9120 (Canada).
Gareth Stevens Publishing's Fax: (414) 225-0377.
See our catalog, too, on the World Wide Web:
http://gsinc.com**

Library of Congress Cataloging-in-Publication Data

Stickland, Paul.
    Places / Paul Stickland.
        p. cm. — (Working)
    Includes index.
    Summary: Tells about different kinds of work and work places.
    ISBN 0-8368-2158-0 (lib. bdg.)
    1. Work environment—Social aspects—Juvenile literature.
    2. Work—Social aspects—Juvenile literature. [1. Work.
    2. Occupations.] I. Title. II. Series: Stickland, Paul. Working.
    HD6955.S836   1998
    331.7'02—dc21   98-13651

This North American edition first published in 1998 by
Gareth Stevens Publishing
1555 North RiverCenter Drive, Suite 201
Milwaukee, Wisconsin 53212 USA

© 1991 by Paul Stickland. Designed by Herman Lelie.
Produced by Mathew Price Ltd.,
The Old Glove Factory, Bristol Road,
Cherborne, Dorset DT9 4HP, England.
Additional end matter © 1998 by Gareth Stevens, Inc.

Gareth Stevens series editor: Dorothy L. Gibbs
Editorial assistant: Diane Laska

Printed in Hong Kong

1 2 3 4 5 6 7 8 9 02 01 00 99 98

PLACES

Paul Stickland

Gareth Stevens Publishing
MILWAUKEE

Inside a garage, mechanics fix cars and trucks. Outside, people stop to buy gas for their automobiles.

As trees are cut down in forests, new ones can be planted to replace them.

At a day care center, you can paint and
play and listen to stories.

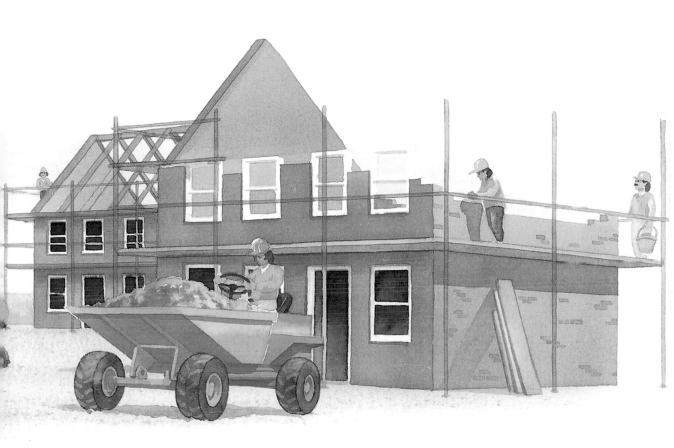

Building new houses is a big job.
Workers need big tools, such as ladders,
wheelbarrows, and concrete mixers.

A farmyard has animals, tractors, and
tools in it. There's lots of work to do.

10

At a hospital, doctors and nurses help
people who are sick or hurt get better.

Harbors are safe places for boats.
People work there and have fun, too.

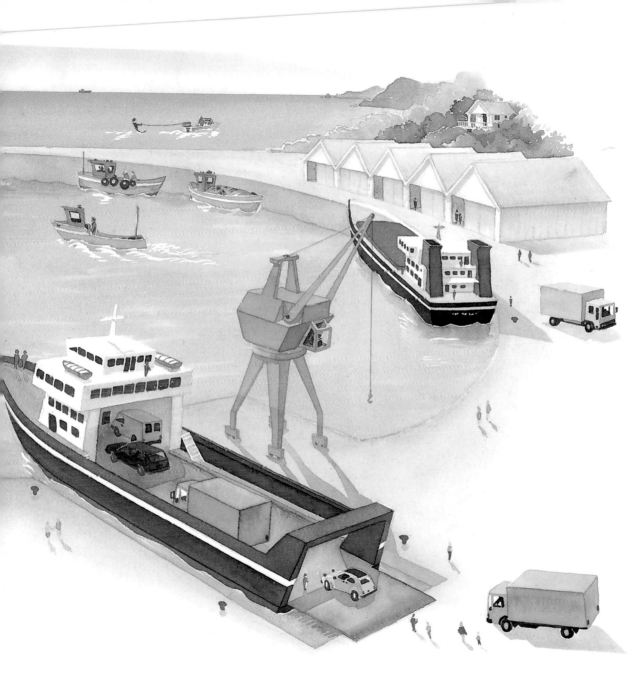

Shops sell many different things.
This shop sells toys and games.

Wouldn't it be fun to work
in a toy shop?

GLOSSARY

automobile — a vehicle with an engine and four wheels that carries passengers and things from one place to another.

concrete — a mixture of cement, sand, gravel, and water that gets very hard when it dries.

harbor — a protected area of water where boats stay when they are not going anywhere.

mechanic — a person who uses tools to fix engines and other machines.

tractor — a large, heavy vehicle that has very big wheels and a powerful engine and is used to pull farm machines.

wheelbarrow — a boxlike cart that has only one wheel at the front and is pushed by hand.

INDEX